How to Text a Woman

Discover How a Girl Wants You to Text Her even If You're Shy and Never Run Out of Things to Say

Sabrina Schuman

Table of Contents

Introduction

So you have exchanged numbers or social media with a girl. Now what?

Most guys get too caught up on random bullshit texting rules the dating community has made up. The PUA's say you should wait 24 hours to text the girl, you shouldn't put emojis, and your text should contain perfect grammar, etc. It's all bullshit.

It doesn't matter if you take 24 hours to text her or 24 minutes. The fact is she will get the text either way. It's what you text that is more important. My personal preference is to text a girl after 7pm. This is when people aren't usually busy. If you text a girl throughout the day, expect her to reply late since people are busiest throughout the day. They go to work, they do their groceries, they might go to the gym, etc.

I wouldn't recommend texting a girl on a Friday or Saturday night because most women go out on these days. If you text her on a Friday night, you are subconsciously saying, "I have nothing better to do on a Friday night, so I am texting you." If you really want to text her on a Friday night for whatever reason, I recommend you start the conversation off with "I am at this club and..." or "I'm getting ready to go out ...". This shows that you aren't sitting alone at home waiting for her to text back like a needy guy.

Purpose of Texting

The main purpose of texting is not to have a long deep conversation with the girl. The only purpose of texting is to get the woman out on a date. If you're in high school, then sure, text the girl and try to have a conversation with her over text, but if you're a man, you should use texting to get her out. Leave the conversation to when you meet up.

This doesn't mean, however, that your second text should be you setting up a date. You shouldn't start a conversation; you should, however, tease and be flirty with her through text. This will give her all the positive emotions she needs to agree to meet up with you. More on that later.

The First Text

Many guys stress over the first text and sit there endlessly thinking of the perfect first text. The first text is the most important. If the girl is attractive, then you are most likely not the only guy texting her. You are most likely the only non-needy guy texting her. You must send a low investment text that doesn't end in a question mark to show that you aren't like all the other needy guys. What do I mean by low investment text?

A low investment text is a simple text which you didn't have to put a lot of thought into. You don't have to send the "perfect text."

Avoid asking a question in the first text. Instead, text a statement. If your first text has a question mark in the end, then the girl will feel obligated to text back. If, however you send her a simple statement, she can choose to ignore it. This is a perfect way to see if the girl is interested or not.

There are times where a girl will ignore your text even if you had a great interaction. When this happens, guys get confused as to why they do this. The reason is because of their emotional drives. Have you experienced a scenario where you are texting a girl, and she takes a while to reply to your text, but once you are in an argument with her, her replies are almost instant? This is because of her emotional drive.

When you were interacting with a girl, you would have given her positive emotions and kept her interested. The next day, though, when you text her, her emotions might be flat. If they are, she won't feel the urge to text you back and will probably forget to text you later. Even if she had the best interaction with you last night, if she isn't feeling it, she won't text you back.

There are also texts that you should not send. The worst one is "Hey, it's John from the bar last night. I was wearing a red shirt, remember me?". This is the neediest text you could possibly send the girl. Sure it seems sweet and innocent, and you might be thinking if she was drunk the night before, she might not have remembered you, but this text screams, "Give me validation." Instead, you should send your statement or a reference to something you talked about in your interaction and then just add your name at the end.

Instagram

If you are going to text a girl through Instagram or other social media, you have the advantage of sending photos and videos. You can always start the conversation by sending her a funny photo.

Sometimes I like to send a funny 4-second video. I have a specific video I send which always makes me, and everyone I show it to, laugh. You can be sure the girl laughed at the video if she replies. Not only does sending a funny video separate me from all the other guys it also gives her positive emotions that she associates with me. If you're stuck, find a short funny video and send her that.

When she is scrolling through her DM's, all she is going to see is needy text messages from guys, and then she will see your message "sent a photo." Women are curious; she will click on it.

Once she laughs, you have just given her positive emotions no other guy has given her on a first text. What is lower investment than a simple funny photo? Again she doesn't have to reply to it, but I bet you she will.

Waiting

When I first started getting women's numbers. I would text them and would just wait. What I have not known at the time is that waiting is the worst possible thing you can do. I would start to overthink and become very negative: "The girl isn't interested," "She is probably talking to other guys," etc.

When you have sent your first text, don't just sit there and wait for a text back. Even if you have been talking for a while, you shouldn't wait for any girl's text back. You need to realize that she has a life too. She could still be at work, in the gym, cooking, at a family gathering, shopping, having a shower, eating, reading, her phone is on mute, driving. There are a million different reasons that may be holding her back from replying to you.

The worst possible thing you could do that will let her lose all her attraction towards you is to keep bombarding her with needy messages until she replies. "Why are you not replying?" "Are you there?" "Why are you ignoring me" etc. These kinds of texts subconsciously tell her, "I have no other women in my life, so I am going to sit here on my phone waiting for you to reply because I have nothing better to do." That doesn't sound very attractive, does it?

Instead, what the attractive man does is goes out and has fun. He lives his life. He doesn't spend hours waiting for a girl he has talked to for an hour to reply to his message. He pursues his hobbies and passion; he reads a book, watches a film, spends time with family and friends, and many more, instead of staring at his phone waiting for a text message that will give him validation.

Now that you know what to text, it is important to know what you shouldn't do when texting a girl.

Paragraphs

If the majority of texts on the screen are coming from you, it shows that you are way more invested than she is. One-sided texting is when you are sending paragraphs and she texting back a one-line text. It shows that you are putting so much effort into starting a conversation with her, but she isn't reciprocating that effort.

If you find yourself sending paragraphs, try to hold back a little and let her invest a bit. Slowly decrease the amount of text you send. Remember, you aren't trying to have a long conversation with her. You are purely trying to get her to meet up with you.

Don't Text Her Every Day

Give her some space. The reason women rarely give out their numbers is to not get bombarded with texts every day, 24/7. Don't text her for a day; give her some space after you have had a little back and forth texting. You give her a chance to miss you even slightly. If you are free to text her every single day 24/7 is says something about how interesting your life is.

Calling

I am not a big fan of calling women. Many guys have success by doing this because it adds a new depth to the interaction. It is better to hear someone's voice rather than read their texts. However, the reason I don't call is that it is a too high-pressure situation for a girl. She could be very insecure and not pick up the phone because "Her voice doesn't sound good" or some bullshit excuse. I know a girl that won't pick up the phone unless she is wearing make-up. The girl might not even have time to talk to you on the phone.

My advice is if the conversation through text is going amazingly and you have both been replying pretty fast, then I suggest you ask her if it's cool to call her first. She won't be hit with that element of surprise and put the phone down because of the pressure. Use a time restriction too.

"I'm going to call you real quick because I don't want to text" or just give her any reason whatsoever. Wait for her to reply "Sure," and then you just call her. During texting, your main purpose is to get her out on a date. When talking on the phone, however, you have the opportunity to have a great conversation since her replies will be instant. After your conversation, you set up the date.

Setting Up a Date

You have been texting back and forth or talking on the phone, and everything is going great. You want to go on a date with this girl.

Asking the girl out may seem slightly intimidating at first, but over time, you will overcome your fear of setting up dates.

While you are texting the girl, you will want to make sure you have given her some positive emotions by either teasing and flirting with her or making her laugh. You will then send a text message saying, "What are you doing later?" or "What are you doing Wednesday night?". Her reply will be similar to one of two replies.

She will either reply with a plan she has set up for later, or she will reply with "Nothing."

If she replies with "I'm going to the cinema later," she is either actually going to the cinema, or she is making up an excuse for you not to ask her out. Either way, don't get butt hurt; you can always try again in a few days. Stay in a positive mood. You don't have to completely end all interactions between you and the girl because she didn't agree to go out with you once.

If, however, her reply is "Nothing," that means she is expecting you to ask her out, and you should do it immediately. Remember, you need to show your dominance. Just like when exchanging numbers, you should never ask the girl out on a date. Instead, say, "Let's grab a coffee Wednesday night." If she agrees, then you can work out the details.

You need to show that you don't go on a date with any woman. You do this by adding a statement that will make her qualify herself. All you have to do is say, "Only if you're cool" or "As long as you don't turn out to be a psycho."

The final text should look like this:

"Let's grab coffee Wednesday night, as long as you don't turn out to be a psycho."

You can see that you qualifying the girl takes the pressure off the situation. If you say, "Do you want to go on a date on Wednesday?" this puts too much pressure on her. With the text above, you show dominance and also take the pressure of her.

There is much more to learn. Keep on reading.

Please note that when I use the word "girl," most of the time, I am referring to a grown woman unless I am speaking in the contest of high school.

NOTES

Chapter 1:

Set Your Mindset for Success

T he question of attraction and seduction depends on the mindset that one has. The mindset, in this case, relates to how one views themselves and others. In essence, one needs to acquire a mentality that will put one in the position to understand himself in relation to the environment around him. This is by having an accurate understanding of yourself, your abilities, and weaknesses. Based on this, you can then begin to figure out how you can use these abilities to influence the environment around you and to make interactions directing them towards your desired objective.

The mindset of a person who wants to be a phenomenal seducer but has been bad at it is that they view themselves as having something wrong in their personality. They think they have a weakness that makes it difficult for them to either draw attraction or get women to acquire a liking for them. They are probably reading this book with the hope that this weakness gets fixed. They believe there is probably some secret formula that one has to use in approaching women and talking to them in order to be successful in seduction.

They also look for validation and think that they have to have women in order to be "conquerors." They do not feel self-sufficient and hence seek to desperately woo women in order to appear cool in the eyes of people. It is as if seduction is a means of proving that they can do this probably better than anyone. Yet when they try it, they fail miserably and hence going back to self-doubt mode.

The thing is, seduction newbies are generally wannabes who are motivated by a wrong mindset. They fall short in the mentality, and hence they cannot be successful with women. They try to be fake by trying the popular methods that peers talk about or the ones they see in the movie. They think that covers up on what they are, yet in reality, they failed at the most important step; the mindset.

The reality is if you view yourself as having weaknesses, whether imagined or real, you make them a reality. You feel limited, and no matter what you do to overcome them, the reality of this thought does not let you be free. Successful people do not entertain a thought that they are inadequate or incomplete. Perhaps because thinking like this does not help. You do not fix yourself, and it is not even tested that fixing yourself will lead to better results. Whatever you perceive as being your nature, you start to become. Better have a positive self-concept, it will call out the best in you, and you probably will feel better about yourself and reduce limitations that can come from the mind.

It is vital to avoid the thought that there is a secret formula for handling women. There is none, as this just flows in the same vein in reinforcing negative self-concept. It makes you jealous. You feed the belief that there is something wrong with you and that success with women requires some magical forces that others have and which you have to get out and acquire. Understand that seduction happens naturally, and you only need to package yourself with the right mindset in order to either trigger it or accurately identify where you can be successful. Attraction is also something natural among people, and sometimes you are focused so much on formulas and thinking about your weaknesses that you cannot realize when an attraction is occurring. Sometimes, men only have to learn how to deal with attraction when it comes their way. Some men become nervous and start following certain formulas and applying routines and rules on every occasion of attraction. If there was a secret formula with seduction, then perhaps so many men would have a dynasty of lovers since using the formula guarantees you success with the woman. However, there is no man who is too excellent with seduction to win every woman that is an object of his lust. Get that out of your mind and know you can evoke attraction as you are, just with a few refinements of your random advances.

Correct Your Mindset

There are no tips that one should purport to give you when it comes to how you handle women. What you need is the ability to be socially intelligent. This is because attraction occurs naturally, and it is not so much something that requires you to fix yourself. You are complete the way you are, and you only need to use what you have in you to make it work for you. What works, for now, may not work tomorrow. Just go through a process of social intelligence.

Social intelligence is just the way you interact in a way that makes your presence memorable. This is by behaving in a manner that makes a woman feel an urge to get closer to you. You must be able to enchant and cause a woman to feel she is special and set apart from others. That means that your interactions should be quite purposeful, although not predictably so. Just learn how to behave, to look, to converse, and to connect.

Learn how women open up to you in a way to give you a chance and how they show rejection. Know how to capitalize on chances through social intelligence. These are all subject to how you interact and what you say. If you are texting, having social intelligence is what will guide you in how you socialize in the online space. Know how to lead a girl in the direction of your advances and have the ability to read signals and adjust or even retreat. Do not be rigid and fixated. Do not have an egotistic mindset that tells you that you must win. Do not try to induce things when they seem to be stuck. When a woman does not seem attracted to you, do not be compelling; hover in the region you are at, applying conscious self-awareness until she opens up to another region or level of interaction. Sometimes, women do not like men the first time. This is due to preconceptions, past experiences, and stereotyping.

You, therefore, do not just show up with your haircut and expect that every woman will be swept off the feet. While it may have been the thing that tipped the balance in your favor on one woman, it may just remind another woman of another man who had similar characteristics and is the biggest regret of her life. That is why seduction and attraction are about learning to let things unfold.

However, understand that as much as there are men who have been famed for having a lot of affairs and who swim in covet of women, no one is universally likable. Do not think that there is something you are going to learn, and then you emerge and make a series of kills and begin to be so successful with seduction. As intimated earlier, there are people whom you naturally piss off, and they even just hate you, and that is naturally occurring just as attraction is natural. It, therefore, does not matter much what you learn in order to make yourself the most seductive man around.

So, What Matters?

You can never be the person that understands what every woman thinks. You have no intelligence to grasp what every woman has gone through in their life just by meeting them. It is possible to understand certain common patterns in the behavior of women, but that does not include comprehending the workings in the minds of a woman that make her see you in the way that she does. Definitely, therefore, you need to be real and not fake it as you are not bound to even correct the way a woman perceives you, even if you say things that fool her.

Additionally, seduction should not impede the fact that it is a natural phenomenon. This means that one should not try to be manipulative or make a fool out of the woman. This only makes you less attractive, and manipulation only evokes hate that is momentarily hidden behind the attraction. Do not try to make a woman start to think you are this when you are that. Fooling her just to take advantage of her or lay her is the greatest demonstration of self-doubt. It is a show that you do not think you can win by being what you are. There is no worse statement of self-doubt than acting to be something that you are not. You cannot be loved when you even cannot love yourself.

Understand Seduction

Women naturally have the disposition of acting like they are disinterested. They will want to appear like they do not like something when they do. That is why seduction is necessary. Seduction is when you use various advances to make the woman finally agree with herself to be involved with the person she deeply knows she wanted to be involved with. This comes through creating a connection that is real. It is about boldly showing who you are and letting her decide that you are just what she wanted. You do not fool, you do not fake it, you tell her subconscious that you are this kind of a man and appeal to it to accept and desire you.

This means that knowing who you truly are is the most important thing that matters. Your mindset should be aware of who you are, and in pursuit to learn how to seduce and attract, it should be a pursuit to understand and get to a comprehensive acceptance of who and what you are. This is what is referred to as finding the self. It is the precise and natural way that seduction goes. That a man, as he is, goes up to a woman and tells her that he wants to mate with her. She then decides to pair with the man or turn it down. It all is in the power of the woman to choose. Or otherwise, it will not be seduction but being forceful. Your part as a man is learning how to model your true self and present it to the woman.

This being the case, one needs to fix one's mindset on what really matters. Think about being the best with presenting your true self. Focus on the only thing that is reliable and which is to be real. The woman will have to deal with it, and you will start to realize just how okay you are. You will realize that you suppressed a lot of excellence and success trying to be what you are not. In creating a great mindset of success, you have to question yourself on various aspects that define you and lead you to discover who you are. The essence of doing this is to know what the girls deal with when you are presenting yourself to them. You will be able to realize sometimes why some girls reject you and what others have difficulty dealing with your kind. Knowing yourself will also help to cut your expectations of how women receive you to size.

When you know who and what you are, you can clearly know what can work and who can deal with you and who is bound to have problems dealing with you and what you are. It will help in ensuring that you direct your efforts to seduce people who are open are likely to be open to you. Not everyone can deal with you, and it can be a show of extravagant expectation to think that everyone has the power to handle you. Go through the process of self-discovery, and you will also learn how to know what kind of a woman she is.

How to Know Who You Are

In the end, make what you want and your aspirations a part of who you are. This is by presenting a persona that is ambitious and which is in the process of transformation. For instance, if you are a sportsman, believe that you are a champion and train in a way that a sportsman does. Handle your issues in life like a sportsman, and that is what women will perceive. Just like Mohammed Ali from the age of 19 regarded himself as the world's greatest, view yourself as a champion, a conqueror, or important. This will build your persona and will elevate you from the levels of pettiness. It will also call out the best from you, and hence you will present the real you in a way that the woman can overlook your downsides. That is the mindset of success, and it will make you do well socially even as you excel in seduction and attraction.

NOTES

Chapter 2:

How to Text Women Online

But before the date is set and you start to flirt on a text, it is necessary to know how to start texting her on social media or after getting her number; this is the first approach. The main thing when texting women you just met is that texting isn't good for types of conversations that "get to know you." Leave such conversations for when you're still together. It is because the words you use are the least important thing in a conversation; the predominant feature is your body language and your tone of voice, and those are absent when you're writing.

During texts, flirt a little and keep it light—a little bit of banter. Don't worry about using emoticons, which lets her know you're playing and messing around. One way to increase attraction is to bring up something the two of you connected over when you met. Jokes work best for this because they put her in a fun and playful space right away.

After the first approach to text and after bantering your way to a healthy level of confidence and friendship, you want to concentrate the conversation on making plans. After all, you weren't asking for her phone number so that the two of you could endlessly sit there, talking. Talk to her about things for which you two share a passion, then plan to go out and do something together. If she is not involved at first, don't worry: she might like you, but not the plans, or she may have something to do legitimately. But if she's shooting down ideas repeatedly, then you're probably better off moving on. Either she is not as into of you as you think, or she has no time to date.

Once you both decide to go on a date, the discussion will turn to logistics entirely; keep it simple, plain and fun. When you have decided on the specifics, such as what you're doing, where, when, and how you're both getting there, you can go back to flirting. Perhaps, the last thing you want to talk about is what you watched on TV or what your childhood was like. For an in-person conversation, there is much to say. Avoid the long conversations about your favorite TV shows and what you think about the job for when you see each other.

How to Start Texting?

The first text should be an introduction rather than going forward with a very generic "hi" text. The first important step is to have a special and exciting introduction. Words can be your friend as well as your enemy. One of the main ways that most guys screw up big time is how they approach. Such guys often start with a "hello or hi" text to play it safe, and that is the reason there is no response. Women yearn for passion and desire. If you want to create a desirable self-image with less, you should be able to say more. Many guys try to break the ice, one which may never have been there! I think it is clear enough that your first text depends very much on the level of interconnection between you two.

Let's take two examples of this:

"Princess, hey ...."

Or

"Hi, Lovely ...."

As you can clearly see, these texts are perfect if you are in a serious relationship or are close enough to tease her. However, if you send these texts to a woman who has not yet got a good understanding of you and your character, you are doomed to flag or fail.

Remember, you're aiming to build passion, desire, and appeal. In other words, the guy should strive to introduce himself elegantly, avoid at all costs stupid phrases and/or openers, and start small talk to build relationships.

Here is one more professional approach:

"Hi (NAME), it was great (experience) ...."

Or

"Hi (NAME), that was a blast yesterday! I was thinking ......"

In many circles, it is believed that starting a text with her name could yield better results.

Since not many do that, the person doing it stands out quickly. This is, not to mention, a very elegant way to introduce yourself, and it doesn't seem weird.

Go for a conversation from here. A great suggestion is to remind her of the event you both experienced in some way- let's say it was a party or concert (Hey Tiffany, the concert was great! I can't believe you did ...). It is very important that a person writes one, maybe two lines, from one to two short sentences, and wait for an answer. Do not make it look needy, and definitely avoid filling the entire chat page with your text messages.

The thing under consideration is the fact that a guy shouldn't spend too much time texting the girl. Remember the event; the guy should ask her if she'd enjoyed it, say next week there's a similar activity going on, and ask her to join him. Something similar might just do the job well. Put in a few more phrases to make it sound like a real little chat about text and then ask her. Try nothing too fancy because the more a person writes, the greater chances of screwing things up.

Women are full of emotion. They are much more emotional than the guys. If you want to grasp a woman's art of messaging, it would be your best bet to bind her to you, to make her emotionally addicted.

The most effective way of attracting and connecting with women is by:

- Sending her funny texts-helps; you break the ice and get the conversation going
- Callback Humor can help you to connect to her in a relatively simple and effective way
- Making her happy-making her emotionally addicted, and attracted to you

First, find something funny and text it to her. If you've got something as easy as a post or GIF or maybe a video and you think it could impress her, go for it. It's a different approach from pickup lines, but it will provoke a new response from her because she never expected it.

The second approach is the "Callback Humor" This simply means referring to the thing you mentioned when you first met her. If you talked about animals and she said she will do anything for little kittens, it's good to send her something about cats. Not only is this something she loves and enjoys, but the chances of getting her text you back are very good.

The last, and the most effective way, is to create the emotions inside her. The guy has to figure out what text can make a woman smile. It is not the same as humor on callback. It is much stronger than that. Indeed, a great tactic would be to start with something that you spoke about at the initial meeting and then apply this step.

To text a girl, you must figure out funny things. However, the goal is not merely to laugh at something dumb and pointless. The main idea will be the filling of the environment with joy and enthusiasm to make her feel more relaxed around. It can be a means to learn how to carry on a conversation over text. In addition, she'll get closer and more attracted to you.

Pickup Lines

Pick (someone) up has been used as slang to have a casual sexual encounter with a person since at least the 17th century. The slang inspired the "pickup" adjective, used to describe a line or rehearsed remark, used to strike up a conversation with a person for romantic or sexual pursuance.

One such instance of pickup line was used in 1979 to describe a line of dialog in the classic 1969 movie Midnight Cowboy when the main character tells a wealthy lady: "Beg pardon, ma'am, I'm new town here, just in from Houston, Texas, and looking for the Statue of Liberty."

The term pickup line spread throughout the 1980s and by the 1990s had become associated with the unadvised efforts of men to talk to women in bars (e.g., "Did it hurt when you fell from heaven?"). Usually, pickup lines start with a question followed by a punch line (for example, "Do I know you? Because you look like my next girlfriend.").

Upon the advent of social media and online dating in the 2000s, pickup lines spread across digital communication. They take the form of a private or direct message to someone on these social media platforms, aiming to draw their attention in setting up a date or talking further.

Mistakes to Avoid

There are some mistakes that a person should avoid as they end up complicating the chances for a date.

- Too Nervous

It matters not if this is your first attempt, or perhaps the tenth that you asked this week. You'll feel somewhat insecure and indecisive about texting for a date or call. This is a common problem in the Arena of Dating. So, if you notice that you're getting nervous and impulsive, the best thing you can do would be to leave the phone, take a few minutes of deep, slow breathing, perhaps drink some water and try to clear your mind. Although this may not take away all the anxiety, it will surely put you in a better position not to screw things up.

- Texting a Girl the Same Day after She Gave the Number

You can do that, of course, but be cautious. Don't try to hurry stuff up. It would be better to ask for a drink or something. Don't rush through the dating process. You go after an emotional attachment, and this is only built up in the long run.

- Texting the Girl's Number after Two Weeks

Even if you feel like you've really been able to connect with her and build the foundation of a relationship, if you write her one or two weeks later, you'll find out that the passion is dead.

- Do not Over-Text

Text ideas are to provoke curiosity and take her out on a date and not a forum for discussion. In fact, the more you're writing to her, the greater her chance of seeing you as a texting buddy and not as a potential future boyfriend.

- Speaking of Her as a Guy

That's exactly how you're supposed to text a girl once you've got her number, like a man and not a woman. The thing that surprises people is how softly most people seem to converse in person as well as face to face. You're the man; you're supposed to be the boss, the one with confidence, the alpha male talking his talk and walking his walk. Nonetheless, from observations, no one behaves like that next to someone.

Double-check your grammar and spelling, for example. No girl worth dating will be interested in a guy who can't even write an entire sentence right. Then, be a little better. Being sweet, loving, and compassionate is one thing, and not being able to stand up for yourself and agree with all that is happening to you is a whole other.

- Don't pay Attention to Her

The girl is there to "fill a gap" in your life and not to make it in it. Some people might have a hard time understanding it, but you have your own life and responsibilities. And you have to pay attention to them.

Don't text her constantly. This way, you say directly that you don't have anything going on in your life, and you're thinking about her all day. This ends up with her being more distant and avoids replying to your texts. It is one thing to give the attention needed and another to be obsessed with her like a creep.

- Useful Compliments

A good compliment can secure a home run for you, while a bad one may break your chances in a moment. You should stick to a casual way of talking. Especially if this is your first text since you were given her number, avoid compliments, especially as initial text conversation openers.

It is important to note that compliment has the whole purpose of being sudden, provoking, and sounding genuine.

- Copy Her Style

If you wonder about an appropriate way to email her, you can do the easiest thing, just mimic her style of writing. You may want to mirror the way she interacts with you in order to share the same atmosphere.

- Being Too Sexual

It would be a bad idea to over-sexualize the conversation. Now, a thin line exists between what you can do and what is acceptable. In reality, women love teasing. It is all good to be playful while still being able to provoke passion and emotion, even lust.

There should really be a sort of connection between the two of you, which should be both physical and mental. This is what real relationships are built on, after all.

Nevertheless, guys mistakenly overdo the talking or, in this case, texting in their attempts to carry the message.

Telling her a dirty joke or something of that sort is one thing and totally different from flirting with her always. When she gets the impression that you are only interested in her because you want to use her for your own satisfaction, then your chances suddenly drop to nil.

- Going Across the Board

Even if you think you've planned and organized everything and everything falls perfectly in line, there's always a risk that maybe she'll be busy, maybe she won't want to date you, or she doesn't have any feelings towards you. Both of these circumstances are normal and can happen. Therefore you have to pay close attention to what you say and do.

If your plan hasn't worked out for some reason and you are being rejected, just say something like "All is fine" and get off your phone right away. Do not pressure her in the chat or badmouth or ask her to go out with you.

The fact that she now doesn't want to go out with you doesn't necessarily mean she won't go out in the future with you. It clearly shows you need to develop more emotional appeal before you can take her out.

NOTES

Chapter 3:
The Approach

The correct strategy of approaching women remains a contentious issue for men to date. As such, it is not clear which methods are the most effective and which aren't. This is because of relatively split opinions on the matter. Some people deem the direct approach as the most effective and claim the indirect approach is evasive and time-wasting. Others support the indirect approach where the man usually hides his intentions in disguised behavioral manifestations towards the woman and appears as if he is not even out to hit on her at all. It is therefore important to explore these approaches for purposes of comparison.

Direct Method

This method is usually coming out and declaring your intentions to hit on a woman in no uncertain terms. The proponents of this approach think that it is the most effective and ensures time is not wasted. They also feel that it does not dig so much into one's dating abilities and can be affected by anyone. They claim that the indirect method only raises a buffer that makes it impossible for one to progress his advances at the girl.

Whenever you come out and try to engage a girl in a conversation, she is not daft as not to start analyzing you. Even if you claim to have misdirected a text, she will have to analyze it, and she perceptively can already tell that you probably are approaching her.

There indeed are girls who are oblivious and do not even realize what the man is up to and only end up finding themselves victims of circumstances. However, when you act like you are not interested in her, she probably is aware of it the whole time and can think of you as being pansy.

With this approach, it is required if a man to be clear about his intentions and purpose to be impressive from the first minute. That as a man, you get out and have a glow on you that can naturally evoke admiration and trigger desire from the woman. If it is texting, use every opportunity she allows you from the first minute to be purposeful and to impress. Do not engage in idle texting with a girl as she will only relegate you further into a place where you will not be able to break through to her again.

Those supporting this approach feel a woman should not be allowed a lot of time to know your vulnerabilities and weaknesses before you already have won her over. That immediately you encounter her and decide that she is worth hitting on, you gauge the chances of how she will receive you. Once your perception tells you that she is open to you, do not go beating around the bush. She will also show you already whether she wants you to go on. That this will save you a lot of moments of uncertainty and possibly make you lose your chances in case she is taken by another swift guy while you continue buying time engaging in false disinterest.

The reason why men can be afraid of this approach is the fact that they fear rejection. They, therefore, want to coil around and find a way of being accepted completely. However, using this approach assumes that nothing you do can change the girl's mind about you if you have not impressed the first time. That the first impression determines how the girl will perceive you for the longest time, and you can have a hard time changing that. If she shows some interest and allows you close to her, it is supposed to be taken advantage of no matter what the result will be. If she is not into your advances, waiting will not help it. You will only be delaying the rejection, and hence you will not realize the worth of having waited.

There is some degree of defiance with the people who use this strategy. They are undeterred by rejection, particularly because if it is online, it is a girl they do not know. They have no time to play games and idly engage in purposeless talks. The man goes straight to the point and clearly shows that he is out to hit on her. If the girl does not buy it, they move on to the next girl they are texting.

Besides, some girls detest insincerity and acting out. She may like you for all the reasons and hate you for not being able to stand up to yourself and tell yourself to go out and get what you want. They may associate it with an unstable personality, and if she likes you so much, she may make it difficult for you to ever approach her. So you will be kept in a friendship zone, or if it is texting, she may not allow you to get her to a meet-up. She thinks you are not confident and have a lot of self-doubts which is an anti-seducer and a show of weakness that may just not be what she is looking for in the man.

This approach, however, does not apply to everyone at all. Particularly for texting a girl, it may work, but in very few circumstances. You should not be too forward with your intentions in such a way that you overwhelm her. A girl has got to be allowed time to express herself and understand why she is wanted. Besides, some girls may deem it rude and think you have a compromised perception of who they are. She may be interested, but she may think you are making her appear cheap. It, therefore, still requires you to be perceptive and understand the girl you are going out to.

If it is a girl you have a history of and who has any idea of who you are, it will probably work when you are direct. Assume it is a girl you have been coincidentally meeting on several occasions in the commuter train and have been doing some non-verbal communication; she may have some preparedness. You could walk up to her and ask for her number.

You can then go straight to the point here. You will text her and introduce yourself. You could then straight away ask about a possible evening out since you already have an idea what time she is out of work, and you are sure she should be just about able to make it.

Another advantage of this approach, aside from simply saving time and the trouble, is what it makes the girl think of you. It somehow comes out as a typical masculine expression, and while it may come out rough, the girl may feel you are confident and sure. It is also a bold expression of desire that the girl feels quite flattered for. That you walked across the street and stood up to her to say she is attractive is deeply complementing. Chances are that she has not had that happen to her before, and she may not going to have it happen to her so many times in her life. So on a text message, you can also be that abrupt but careful because she has no idea of who you are. However, texting her for the first time and saying that you could not hold it back and that there is no better time, place, or platform to let her know how you find her attractive will get her thinking.

However, it is also disadvantageous, as already explained earlier. It is a high risk even when its rewards are equally high.

Indirect Approach

This approach is used by a lot of men, particularly given the risks that are associated with the direct approach. In this approach, the man lays low and, in some instances, sends mixed signals. It has already been mentioned that being direct can make you shoot yourself in the foot and bring to an unprecedented what would have been a promising interaction with a girl. When using this approach, the goal is to create a basis for the attraction between you. Sometimes, women may not directly get attracted to a man until time has passed.

For instance, you hear a new song played on the radio, and you do not think it is great. Then you listen to it the second time it is played, and you still do not understand why the song you don't even like has to still be on air. Then you later go out for a karaoke night. Then the song is sung, and you find yourself up and jamming to it alongside other people.

That is how attraction also works. It may not happen immediately but can be evoked with familiarity. Some of the reasons that ladies do not like men are because of the preconceptions they have. When a man is dressed in a certain way, the girl initially thinks that he not interesting and exciting. Going to her at this stage is bound to attract a rebuff. However, take time, let her interact with you, and discover that the exact opposite is true. What is ever so good with women is when their preconceptions are challenged. If she thought the man to be a bore and the man becomes quite exciting, she feels more drawn to him.

As a man, I take it that you are supposed to have a plan on how to handle a woman. This should involve planning and strategizing, and that means you need an approach that will allow you to execute the plan. This will minimize the risks and help you plan, reposition and ensure you are quite accurate.

Chapter 4:

How to Get Her Number

Y ou've been talking a few minutes, and she seems like she's into you. But will she give you her phone number? Will she go out with you?

First of all, you need to be in the mindset that, of course, she will. She has given you no reason to think she wouldn't, so keep that positivity.

You have to believe that every woman you are interested in will give you her number. It's not arrogance. It's just a feeling of positivity and abundance. You are an intelligent, good-looking, and interesting guy, so there is no reason she would not want to get to know you. If you operate on this level, you will radiate confidence.

So, how do you move the conversation to a point where you can get her number?

Small Talk to Real Conversation

The biggest trick to moving from small talk and casual conversation to something more meaningful is to validate their interests and pull them into a deeper conversation.

What all this means is: find the small things in what they are saying or doing that can be seen as important by both of you.

Let's try a hypothetical situation:

You are at a coffee shop, and you notice a beautiful woman waiting for her coffee right next to you. You give her a smile; she smiles back, and you have some good eye contact. She comments on your shirt color, and you thank her.

Right as your coffee comes, you notice she has a nice bracelet that is very unique. You comment that it's really cool. She smiles, thanks you, and says she got it when she was traveling in Asia. You say that sounds cool, and she smiles, says goodbye, and leaves.

What happened?

You had the perfect opportunity to turn casual small talk into a much deeper conversation. She gave you the perfect opening when she said she got her bracelet in Asia.

That's the opportunity to take a bit of small talk information and turn it into a conversation that is meaningful. Travel is a perfect opportunity. When people take a trip, especially to another country or part of the world, there is going to be an emotional connection. They are going to be happy to share.

If you had said something like, "Asia? I've never been there. What was that trip like?" you would have opened up the door for a longer and more real conversation.

Look for those nuggets in small talk that can open women up.

Asking for the Digits

Before you ask, check for these things.

Check for that ring on her left hand. Make sure you didn't miss it. You don't want to realize you are hitting on a married woman. All good?

Did she say she's seeing someone? Some guys think that if she's got a boyfriend, she's still up for some fun. She's not married.

I think this is disrespectful and makes you less of a man. If you had a girlfriend and some guy tried to make a move, how would you react? It's one thing for her to say she has one, but if you know, back off. Treat her the same way you would want your own girlfriend treated.

Assume It's Going to Happen

Be confident that you two are going to go out and have fun. Don't say, "Is it ok if I ask you out?" You don't need permission to ask her. Just ask!

Be specific. Say, "Would you have dinner with me?" or "Maybe let's have dinner." Assume that she's just had a great conversation, and of course, she's going to want to see more of you! Come up with a day as soon as you can.

Snap a Picture

If you are somewhere interesting, offer to snap a photo and text it to her. You'll get her number. If getting her number doesn't seem right at the moment, offer to post it on Instagram and ask what her profile is and follow her. Then tag the photo and contact her online.

Use What You Have Learned

I will bet you that she has provided you with at least a dozen different ways to ask her out, but you didn't even realize it.

As she tells you things about herself, look for the information. What has she said she has wanted to do but never had the chance? You probably aren't in a position to take her to Paris, but if she said she's never had French food, ask her out to a French dinner. Does she want to see the new award-winning dramatic film coming out next week?

Say you should go together.

During your conversation, you are getting to know her, and the truth is she is telling you exactly what to do. She has told you her likes and dislikes, so you just need to figure out the best one for her right then.

Make sure it's one you can do right away. If she says she's excited about a movie coming out in six months, not a good idea to pursue that. You don't want to wait six months for a date. Or if there's a club or restaurant she's interested in but hasn't opened yet, don't wait. Find your opportunities!

Topics to Avoid

- Your Exes

While it is common to find common ground with your past relationships, this can turn negative pretty quickly. Instead of having a positive experience and enjoying each other, you are going to bring up bad memories on both sides. Commiseration is not stimulating conversation that turns people on.

- Personal Trauma

Unless you're talking to this woman at some sort of support group, try to avoid any discussion of past personal trauma until you've known her for a while. (And if you did meet her at such a group, remember to focus on healing first and being part of a support system for your fellow survivors, not getting laid by the cute girl by the snack table.) Trauma can be a real bonding agent, and women want you to be open with them about your feelings—later in the relationship. Even mental health problems, something which we should always try to normalize so that people won't be afraid to seek help, should wait until you two are more comfortable with each other.

Until then, don't use this to propel a conversation, even if she provides you with the perfect opening. You don't want to scare her away.

- TMI

Do you recall a commercial where the woman is on a first date with this guy, and when the guy mentions how awkward first dates can be, she replies, "Yeah, like my constipation"? You would hope that this commercial is just an exaggeration meant for comedic effect, but you'd be surprised. Some people really do share way too much in their first conversation with someone, especially if they get nervous or run out of things to say. Avoid this at all costs.

Obviously, bodily functions are off-limits. So is bragging about your sexual prowess or how hung you are. Like I said before, talk about love and passion, not sex. Besides, those organs are just not something women—or anyone—want to hear about when they first meet you. Gross.

Remember, use innuendo, but be subtle. Don't be TMI.

- Politics and Religion

Eventually, this can become a wealth of conversation, but at first, be very careful bringing up politics and religion until you know where both of you stand.

Don't editorialize or go on about your personal beliefs, especially religion. If you go to church, say so but don't make her think you are highly religious and almost became a priest. If you aren't religious, don't lie and say you are, instead just touch on it, saying you're not that religious. If it gets to the third and fourth date, then start talking about these things. But not yet.

- Sports

She may love sports, but the vast majority of women don't want to talk about it all the time and definitely not the breakdown of box scores or how you can remember the entire line-up of the 2016 World Champion Chicago Cubs baseball team.

She's probably going to ask if you watch sports and which ones. Tell her the truth, but don't dwell on it. She's trying to find out if it's such a dominating thing that it would potentially take away from the time you two might spend together.

Ask her if she watches or enjoys sports. Often women connect sports to emotional events, like family outings to games as a kid or watching football on Sundays with her dad.

You, however, most likely connect it to certain events, like the once-in-a-lifetime comeback you watched or an amazing play or the time a player got injured, and they showed it over and over on replay.

So, find her connection. And never belittle other sports because they aren't the ones you watch. Don't start saying how stupid golf or soccer is because you might just find out she does it every weekend. Even if you have rival teams, don't belittle her for cheering for them. A bit of good-natured teasing is fine, but make sure to keep it in check.

Last Resort

If you don't think anything will work and you don't know what to do...

Just ask her!

Just come right out and ask, no matter what the conversation has been like. You don't have to lead up to it. If you felt like there was a connection, then just ask her.

Sometimes you just need to take a chance.

Chapter 5:

From Small Talk to Deep Conversation

When you start talking to a girl, it is best to let the conversation flow naturally and not be too controlling. Non-confrontational interaction is a good way of approaching a girl and allows her to meet you where you are at. It also makes sure that she will not be uncomfortable with your advances. The best way to do this is by being talkative, as this will give people confidence.

It is easier to have a conversation if you are in a group rather than one-on-one. A group gives you more talking partners, and hence if you are not good in conversation, you can just choose to talk to another person as it seems natural. Moreover, when you are part of a group, there is more structure on how the conversation should flow.

When using small talk, the trick is not to make it useful but rather, it just helps us connect with each other. It creates a good first impression, and a conversation that is too heavy can put a person off. In a group, it is better for you to speak in the others' pauses rather than speak under your breath. It gives the impression that you are comfortable enough to start chatting with people you just met. This is also the time to show your confidence as you are relaxed and find out whether she has any interesting friends.

When approaching strangers, do not go straight up to her and start talking about her job and other personal stuff. Use small talk initially and then gradually transition to deeper conversation. You can start by asking about people's names, where they are from, and how everybody met, for example. Let the conversation flow naturally in order for you to get carried away with it.

On the other hand, do not rely on small talk too much as this is just useless banter and may make you come across as a bore. It is also important not to overdo being funny as this will only make the atmosphere awkward. Ideally, you would want to end up in a situation where there are no pauses during your conversation or when speaking with her. You should be careful though, that while you keep her talking, she does not end up answering all questions without your input in a normal conversation. You must also try to make sure that the person or group has enough people in it so that you have someone else to go back and speak with.

A good way of getting into a flow so that the conversation flows easily is by using both small talk and deep conversation during a single conversation. Just before you end your conversation, let the other person go first by commenting on something you did not mention earlier and thank her for the conversation. This will show your appreciation as opposed to just leaving without saying thanks. You should also avoid giving her last-minute surprises such as asking her for your number or not letting them finish their meal without letting them know what you are doing next.

If she is single, you should try to start talking about what you like and how you are looking for a relationship that is right and not just one based on physical attraction. You should also initiate the conversation as opposed to she talking about herself to you first or talking about her preferences in men and how she sees herself. The best way to do this is by asking her questions about what she likes in a man without making it sound obvious. For example, ask whether she prefers someone who embraces her or someone who surprises her.

You should also make sure that the conversation doesn't drag on as much when there are several people present. You should ask questions that keep the conversation going or things that let you help in the situation. You should also avoid asking too many questions as this can be seen as difficult and intrusive. This will make women see you as a person who is interested in her rather than a weirdo who is just trying to get to know her.

Introduce the opposite sex to each other, especially if they are not close friends. Doing this helps you break down any tension that may be caused due to not knowing who would talk and what they would choose to talk about. It also gives you time for your conversation with her, and if this goes well, she could introduce you to some of her friends which you could then meet at a later date.

Keep the topics of conversation to what both of you are comfortable with. For example, if you are not interested in sports and she is, do not talk about it. It is alright if you ask her what she likes or what her interests are. This gives her a hint that you are interested in getting to know her more than just finding out whether she knows anything about football. You will find that when it comes to sports, it is so easy for a girl who likes them to bore you with endless statistics and facts that would repulse any man who does not follow up on football or any other sports they like.

Avoid letting the conversation drop while you are out with a girl unless you have just started talking to her. Some men will be quite interested in her and want to get her number or perhaps take her out, but they just get stuck in a position whereby the conversation is coming to an end and then doing nothing about it.

The best way to understand what the other person is feeling is by keeping an eye on their body language. If she looks warm, it means the conversation is flowing well. But if she breaks the flow by asking you a question or handing you the coat she borrowed from you, then this means that she isn't feeling comfortable with what you are saying.

You should also be careful not to say anything that might make her feel uncomfortable or cause her to feel like she was being judged by you unconsciously. You will, however, find that most girls will show a reaction in situations like these and not just let it slide as it might hurt her feelings. If this happens, you should apologize and try to make her feel better. You should also try to avoid saying things that may be offensive to the girl even if they were not meant as such.

This point is important, especially when you have just met a girl for the first time and have not had time to get to know her very well or she has had no time with you either. Therefore, knowing how she feels through her body language can help you avoid making mistakes later when she becomes more comfortable with you.

When in conversation, both parties must be comfortable with what the other person is saying. This is important as if one person feels uncomfortable with how the conversation is going or what the conversation partner is saying, it can make the other person feel uncomfortable too.

It is important when having a conversation that both parties are listening actively and not just waiting for their turn to talk again. This is because when she is talking, she is not only trying to give you a message but also trying to see if you are paying attention to what she is saying. Therefore, when she feels that you are not paying attention, she may get distracted from the conversation, and as a result, an uncomfortable situation may arise between the two of you. Hence it is important that you listen actively by asking questions or making comments throughout the whole conversation so that she can feel engaged instead of just feeling like she has to talk all the time. You should also try to avoid too many interruptions while speaking, especially when it doesn't seem necessary and just for your own benefit, mainly so that the conversation can flow properly.

NOTES

Chapter 6:

Texting Tips to Get More Dates

A lot of guys do text girls but come out sloppy and sometimes purposeless. A man just takes the number and starts circumventing and going round in circles until he becomes notoriously a bother. Some men also have aims for texting, yet they cannot get them across through the text. Aimless texts that do not seem to be tied to a purpose do not elicit emotion or grip the girl with a sense of awe.

You should know that a man can only have two objectives to text a girl, that is noted as the sister, business partner, or client; to either establish friendship through the building of rapport or to get the girl to agree to a date. However, the core aim and the paramount one is that you should be able to get the girl to meet up with you. There are guys who come out with a maligned objective of just hanging around with endless texting and hop back and forth to a fortunate date with her. This is quite timid, redundant, and could veer into the quarters of irritation to the girl.

When you do not have an objective, the girl starts to wonder if you do not have someone else to tell the sort of things you are texting her with. The girl wants you to come out focused and sharp, ensuring you that nothing gets messy. Do not let your target get lost in the process of engaging in chit-chat. So that means that do not mix up texting her to establish a relationship base, perhaps as a precursor to friendship and texting her to just secure a date. If you want to meet her, you want to meet her and focus on making that happen.

Avoid circumventing around your goal as you will confuse yourself. You will find yourself sending too many texts to which no replies will be forthcoming. Come out bold and courageous. Appear sure and exude confidence that that is what you are, and it gets you the results you want. Having known the objective of texting, then you can focus on the matter in the texts.

Text Warm and Cold

There are two forms of texting in light of the objectives stated above. Cold-texting and Warm-Texting. When you text a girl that has an anticipative mindset and is minding you at the moment you text her, that is warm texting. Cold texting is when the girl is probably oblivious to you and has no expectation that you are going to text her.

This distinction is important since you are supposed to know how far you are going to get the girl from in order to be able to put everything set towards attaining your objective on her. You are supposed to tune the way the texts come out to match her level of readiness for you.

Texting A Girl to Drive Towards A Date

When you want to build rapport first, it may take some schedule that can be quite rigorous. Start by texting her for several days to build a base of mutual interest, perhaps. After you have met her and she shares her contact with you, initiate communication through text and invite her to some engagement for the sake of socializing or mingling. You will, therefore, need to keep the conversation following the approaches of keeping a conversation going. However, do not take it into over a week before you are already at the point of arranging for a meet-up. So typically, you will be texting her with a date slated to come in a few days, maybe five days away.

But better for you if you could not engage in rapport building. This is unless you perceive the girl to be one that requires you to take her through such an adventure. When you have secured the number, proceed to your main goal already without heeding the urge of trying to win her. This requires you to stop selling yourself as a brand like you are an item. The point just goes straight to making the girl go out with you. Obviously, rapport building will fall into place by itself.

You should first come out warm and with charm in your texts. This is in order for you to lower the girl's defenses and avoid alerting her to be suspicious and resistant. Then ensure that you have something of value that you appear to be offering. Whatever that is could be imagined or illusionary, but it should be able to get the girl drooling with curiosity. It could also simply the fun thing that she desires to be doing, which is to meet you. Only that she is laying back to let you lead her there. So, a girl will text some messages that may be destructive such as, "How is your day going?" Answer but ensure that she does not get you entangled into sideshows that sidetrack you. Keep steering towards your goal regardless of what you are talking about.

The text thread could appear like this;

Man: Lisa, hello! I am thinking we could work on creating time to get some snacks. Could this weekend be appropriate for you?

Girl: The weekend is usually free apart from my routine to spring clean the house. What is for dinner?

Man: arranging to cook. So, you could do the cleaning and then you are free. It sounds workable for me. We do this at 3 pm. I know you are going to like it at the Pop Club.

Girl: Looks hurried, but will set me for it.

Man: I look forward to it, see you on Saturday.

See how the meet-up comes through quite fast and ready. It only had to take being focused on the goal. When she asked about dinner, the guy does not switch subject to discussing food and how it is going to be cooked or what is going to be cooked. You may risk being supped out of all seductive energy when she entangles you in questioning or succeeds in getting you to overexpose yourself to her, which makes her judge you. Push your agenda and appear clinical as opposed to being blunt and unfocused.

A strategy could be to use the first meeting to suggest that you could get out a bit before you even take her number. This is something that can make the process a lot easier than waiting to pursue a date fresh on text. The good thing here is that asking for the date first before getting physical with her makes the girl have more readiness for you. It just even makes your next move of asking for her number easier as that is the only way that the date will get set up.

You have an opportunity to ask the girl to go out with you in person, and you should not squander it. Do not wait for the text-only, as perhaps she could think you are not confident enough to just get out and get what you want. So, seize the moment to get things started on an auspicious note. For instance, when you are conversing, in person, with her and she is explaining something, you steer it to your aim;

Girl: (in the course of a conversation at the place you have met) .... I had to really get out of the place and save her from an awkward moment. She was almost freaking out.

Man: Haaa, you mean? That was so intuitive of you.

Girl: we girls feel nervous when awkward moments happen, so I just had to be a great friend.

Man: and on that note, I think we are going to go back to the club; your fun was cut short when you left. How is your weekend looking?

Girl: well, that will depend. I will need to confirm.

Man: That is fine, so what is your number? I will text you.

Girl: 5672....

How hard was that? You are immediately working on your objective at the first meeting, and the texting only comes later as a follow-up. She will now not be surprised when you text her, and you are not concerned about rapport building but rather remind her to confirm her availability for the Sunday date. This can help you seduce a girl in the way that you expend lesser efforts yet get back huge rewards. In fact, going y this, I could demand you to right away go into your contacts to delete all of the numbers of girls you took and whom you did not suggest to go out with at the first meeting.

Icebreaker Text

Also, focus on ensuring you are good at breaking the ice by avoiding taking too long before you can text the girl. The longer you hesitate or "dilly dally" in sending the text, the weirder it will just get for you. She keeps wondering if you will send her a text at all or simply moves on and forgets having met and exchanged contacts with you. You also start to pile up thoughts in your head as you overthink that will naturally make you come out rather awkward.

The way out is to execute the icebreaker. This will immediately set you free as your fear of how the conversation will go has been dispatched. Having sent the icebreaker text, it imparts into the girl some sense of anticipation that you will probably text her further in the coming moments. It will also help you that when you eventually text her for a cat, you will not have the need to start saying who you are, and hence you have a head start in getting busy to pursue your objective. An example of a text to break the ice is;

Man: I just had a great time with you in the lobby. I did not notice the time pass. Nice hooking up, your latest friend :) Hudson

Or

Man: It has been an exciting time talking to you. Steve here.

You could keep it as short as possible just to ensure she does not already get thinking she has taken your breath away. You are being careful to also not appear needy and desperate. The icebreaker will appear quite infectious yet portray you as one who is used to meeting new girls, and it is not quite much of a big deal. You are also using a friend to tease her a bit and get her attention. She will be pondering if you mean to be interested or if you are neutral towards her. She hopes you come out to clear this confusion. However, if you sense that the girl is already on your radar and likes you already, avoid using "friend." This is for the girl who is flattered that you gave her attention and that you have class over her. Do not use "friend" to make her feel snubbed or despair that she can't have you.

Chapter 7:

Examples of Text Conversations

Men call women who give them their phone numbers but avoid meeting them in person are flakes. Numerous men's forums on the internet are dedicated to flakes and how to prevent flaking. Given our problem-solving nature, it is not surprising that we men have come up with a variety of ways to account for the impact of flakes on our love lives. Some men schedule dates with two or more women at the same time to account for the possibility of one of the women flaking on him. Others use a variety of ethically worrisome texting tactics to coerce women into not being flakes. While I applaud these men for their ingenuity and fighting spirit, I think they missed the boat by not addressing the crux of the problem.

Women flake on men because men fail to demonstrate their high sexual market value during texting exchanges with them. If these men were strategic about using their texts to playfully and effectively communicate to these women the fact that they are masculine men who have high social status and are preselected by women, women would not flake on them. In fact, ever since I figured out how to emphasize these attributes about myself in my communications with women, no woman has flaked on me.

Use text messages to subtly communicate your high sexual market value.

Thus, you must subtly imply that you are a high-status man instead of explicitly stating it in your text messages. Being terse, gently, and playfully disqualifying her statements, making her wait for your responses to her text messages for at least as long as she makes you wait for her responses to your text messages, giving her directives, and occasionally providing approval help create this implication in her mind.

Also, you must implicitly suggest that you have other sexual options instead of explicitly stating it. A great method to accomplish this is by demonstrating that you are indifferent to getting her approval and not concerned about her losing interest in you. Indifference can be shown in a variety of ways, such as using poor grammar and punctuation, ignoring her questions, teasing her playfully, and responding without emotion to her actions.

Exercise caution when texting women to avoid triggering their auto-rejection mechanisms

Demonstrating a high sexual market value via texting requires one to be cautious as well. If a woman feels that you are too good for her, she will suspect that one or more of the following statements is true and try to confirm her suspicions:

- You want to pump and dump her.
- You will be an unfaithful boyfriend.
- Your interest in her is not genuine, and you have ulterior motives.
- You are actually not as great as she thinks you are.

In her mind, the following question is of paramount importance –

why would such an attractive man, who can be with women who are more attractive than me, be so interested in me? The longer this question remains unanswered in her mind, the more likely a woman is to auto-reject you when you fail to escalate your interaction with her to the next level. When she auto-rejects you, she will take any of your minor flaws and blow them up out of proportion to convince herself that you are not good enough for her. The more insecure a woman is about her appearance, the more often this emotional self-defense mechanism rears its ugly head.

To avoid being auto-rejected by a woman during texting interactions with her, you must never explicitly say anything negative to her in your text messages. Needless to say, any sort of teasing or flirting must be done very playfully. If you need to punish her bad behavior, you can ignore her texts and not respond to them for a pre-determined period of time, make your texts terser and/or cryptic, or respond to her texts very erratically.

Avoiding auto-rejection will be especially important for you if you are an attractive man because you can trigger a woman's auto-rejection mechanism by simply making a few jokes at her expense. Let us look at a very detailed example of a text message-based conversation in which I subtly communicated my high sexual market value to a woman without triggering her auto-rejection mechanism. My comments are italicized.

S: I learned how to boil water last year, and I'm pretty proud of it! Far from sashimi, but hey, I'm trying lol 3:42 PM

A day later

Me: I bet YOU don't even need to turn the gas on for that. 3:47 PM

60

I responded a day later, showing I was unafraid of her losing interest in me. Also, I teased her, implying that I have high social status.

S: Sure don't! Just bought an electric kettle. 3:48 PM

Me: Well, played 3:48 PM

I gave her my approval, implying that I have high social status.

S: How was ur weekend? Go on crazy dates again? 3:49 PM

Me: No crazy ones, missed a flight to the Dominican Republic, ended up chilling in Vienna 4:02 PM

I made her wait for my response, implying that I have high social status. Also, I implied that I did go on dates with other women.

S: What?! How the heck did that happen? Oooh, I'd be pissed. Have u been before? 4:14 PM

S: Did the possessive one try to see u again? I'd be like, sorry I'd rather watch paint dry...at least that's my excuse lol 4:15 PM

Me: friend-zoned her, what happened w your nice date? 4:33 PM

I ignored her first question to show my indifference to her walking away. I made her wait for 18 minutes to Pooh show my indifference to her walking away from this conversation. Also, by admitting to friend-zoning a girl for being too possessive, I implied that I have many sexual options.

Me: Shit happens. I fly every week 4:35 PM

I gave a very vague and brief answer to imply that I have high social status.

S: Nice date offered to make dinner last week, but a killer migraine made an appearance, so I canceled. Yikes, I hear ya. Hope u got airline credit. What do 4:41 PM

S: u do that has u flying every week? 4:41 PM

Me: Wow, that's a lot of effort on his part 4:53 PM

I made her wait for my response and ignored her question to show my indifference to her walking away from this conversation. Also, I subtly passed judgment on her date to imply that I have high social status.

S: He's def nice but not feeling a spark. Could be bc this is my first crack at dating since the last guy. Boohoo 5:04 PM

S: I even wore a sexy black dress. 5:05 PM

She sends a picture for me to see.

Me: U have a very mischievous grin 5:20 PM

I complimented her but not about her dress to avoid qualifying to her. Also, I made her wait for my response for 15 minutes to imply that I have high social status.

S: I disagree! Ur mancandy in a suit 5:26 PM

Me: Wow. 5:32 PM

She made me wait for 6 minutes, so I made her wait for 6 minutes. Also, I didn't act all that excited about receiving a compliment from her to show my indifference to getting her approval.

S: Yes. A compliment has been earned...don't get used to it!!! 5:36 PM

Me: I'm printing your text and putting it on my refrigerator. 5:37 PM

I playfully tease her to keep things light and fun.

S: Oh hell no. Not ok! So, when do we get to meet? Something basic like Starbucks...not asking to roll out the red carpet 6:08 PM

Me: out of town M-thurs, next wknd or quick drink tonight? 6:15 PM

Once again, I make her wait for my response to imply my high social status. Also, my response is in line with my being a high-status man who is never too available.

S: I'll be back in the area around 8:30 today...is 9 too late for you? If so, next wknd is totally fine. No rush 6:19 PM

Me: 9 should be fine 6:25 PM

S: Sounds good. Know of a place open past 10? Not looking for a late-night but also don't want to be rushed 6:40 PM

Me: I'll find one. 6:45 PM

S: Cool. Around Vienna/Fairfax is preferred 6:46 PM

Me: I was gonna find a place in SE DC, but ok Vienna/Fairfax it is. 6:47 PM

I take control of the situation like a high-status man while keeping things fun.

S: Lol, you're silly. I'm looking as well. 6:49 PM

Me: Gordon Biersch Brewery at Tyson's corner open till 11, see you at 9 7:28 PM

I don't reply back for about 50 minutes to avoid seeming needy. And, by expecting her to follow my lead, I imply my high social status.

S: Sounds good! 7:32 PM

S: Ok to meet at 9:15? Bus from NY had a slight delay 7:58 PM

Me: K 8:50 PM

I do not respond to her text for about an hour to imply that something or someone more important than her is keeping me busy.

We meet for drinks. She texts me about five minutes after our date ended.

S: Glad we got a chance to meet up! Really enjoyed talking to you. Drive safely, safe travels this week, and get some sleep tonight! 12:22 AM

Me: I had fun too. Just got home. Gnite 12:26 AM

I give no indication of my future plans and use terse wording to imply I might have other, more attractive options.

NOTES

Chapter 8:

Dos and Don'ts in Texting

H ere are guidelines to assist you to up your texting game effortlessly.

DO Text a Girl Quickly

I don't understand guys that see a text from a girl and wait 30 minutes or an hour to reply. If you see a text, reply to it. There is no point analyzing the time it took the girl to text you back so you can take longer to reply. If the girl starts to see a pattern and realize what you are doing, she will discover what an immature, needy guy you are and be instantly turned off.

Dating is about creating connections with one another, having fun, and being flirty with another person. It's not about studying the time it took for the other person to reply.

One of the major downfalls of the "pick-up" and dating community is things overcomplicated for no reason.

It's simple. If you see a text from a girl, you reply to it.

If both of you are replying quickly to each other, you are more likely to have a fun conversation that flows. You will build momentum, which is crucial for when you are ready to ask her on a date.

Remember how we talked about texting her to create emotions? Well, how are you supposed to create emotions if you are texting each other hours apart?

But What If the Girl Is Taking Forever to Reply?

Before you start texting girls, get a life. There will be times where you take a while to reply too, since you have an awesome life.

The girl will notice that you have a life, and your world doesn't revolve around her, which shows independence and self-confidence. It will make her much more attracted to you.

DO Text Her Enough to Get Her Interested

I see many guys try to text as little as possible to show that they are "hard to get." When you start texting a girl you just met, it is natural for you to put more effort than her. You are trying to "prove" that you are a cool guy.

The girl won't be receptive to you straight away because her defense mechanism is up. When girls meet a new guy for the first time, they have this imaginary little shield to protect them. This shield goes up because you are a stranger to the girl. She doesn't know you, which means she doesn't trust you. If she doesn't trust you, she won't flirt with you or show you her true personality.

What you need to do is put effort into your texts to show her that you are a cool, laid-back, light-hearted guy, so her imaginary little shield gets lowered. Once the shield is lowered, that's when she starts letting her personality shine through. That's when she starts flirting back.

Give it time at the start and put in some effort. The girl won't fall in love with you overnight. You need to text the girl just enough to get her interested and build momentum to get her to start thinking about you.

DON'T Use Cheesy Emoji's

There are only two emojis you should use—either the flirty one or the laughing one. All other emojis are pointless.

These are the two most masculine emojis available. Please don't use the monkey faces or kissing emojis. These just make you seem more feminine. If someone was to read your texting conversations and think you are a girl, then you need to ease up on the emojis.

This brings me on to my next point...

DO Use Emoji's Sparingly

The only time you should use emojis is when you are trying to show your true intentions. If you are teasing the girl, then adding a laughing emoji will let her know you are just kidding around.

Do use the laughing emojis sparingly. Don't spam the girl with 7 laughing faces with every reply you send. One is enough, maybe two if what she said was funny. If you start to overuse the laughing face, you won't seem genuine, and it will turn the girl off.

Lastly, please don't use "Haha" or "Lol." You have emoji's available to you; use them.

If you are unsure whether you should use an emoji or not... don't. You can overuse emojis, but you can't underuse them.

DO Tease Her

You should always tease a girl. It shows her that you're not a suck-up and that you don't put her on a pedestal.

Teasing also creates fun, flirty conversations, which is exactly what you want to be doing. You can always use the laughing emoji to show that you are teasing her and that you're not being serious.

Many times I have been in conversation with girls where I would tease them and forget to put a laughing emoji resulting in them thinking I was being serious. The laughing emoji is a lifesaver; use it wisely.

DON'T Text Her All Day

No matter how awesome your life is, you should never text the girl all day, every day, unless the girl is doing the same. I say this because you need to invest just as much as the girl does for a real connection to be created.

Don't text her all day if she isn't doing the same. The girl doesn't want to know every single little detail about your life. It makes you seem desperate. If you're texting her all day, then you are telling her you don't have an interesting life, and your whole world revolves around her.

There is no way you are texting other girls or having a good life if you are texting her 24/7. You should provide her some space to invest; let her miss you a bit. If she knows that every time she turns her Wi-Fi on, or she looks at her phone, she will have a message from you, then that takes the excitement out of texting. You want girls to be eagerly checking their phones, wondering if you have texted them or not yet.

If it helps you, put your phone on silent for an hour while you do something that makes you happy, or work on something that adds value to your life.

I hate it when I'm spending time with my best friend, and every time we start a conversation, we are forced to stop the conversation every two minutes so he can text a girl. Not only does it make him seem more invested in the girl, but it's also annoying because we can't have a real face-to-face conversation with no interruption.

DON'T Always Text Her First

If you're constantly texting first, it shows that you are more into her than she is into you. No matter what you say, if a girl never, if not rarely, texts first, then she just isn't that much into you. I don't care how shy or nervous she is; after a few fun interactions with you, she will text you first if she wants you that badly.

A great way to determine if a girl is into you is to not text her. I realize this statement contradicts the purpose of this book but trust me. After you have been texting back and forth for some time and are having fun, flirty conversation...stop texting her. Don't text her for a few days. If she texts you, that means she is into you. If not, then she might not be as into you as you thought. Always run this test after you create some initial attraction.

Also, no good morning texts. Leave this for when you are in a relationship. Good morning text show that you are way more invested in her than she is in you. It shows that you think about her not only before you go to sleep but right after you wake up.

She is going to think your whole world revolves around her.

DON'T Talk Too Much

Most guys are always trying to think hard for the perfect message to send the girl. Perfection doesn't exist. The same goes for texting.

If you can't think of what to say and see that the conversation is dying down...let it. There is no need for you to keep trying to revive the conversation when you can see that it's not going anywhere.

By not saying anything, you give the girl some space to invest too. If you think it's a good time to end the conversation, end it. Don't be afraid to let go.

DO Use Text to Set Up a Date

The whole purpose of texting is to set up a date with a girl. It is not getting to know her or trying to get nudes from her. It's to get her to go out with you so you can have a face-to-face interaction.

You should always set up dates through text and not through the phone for one simple reason. It is so much easier for the girl to say yes through text than it is through the phone. If you haven't even properly met the girl yet, a phone call will be a bit awkward and might scare her off. Stick with texting.

When you set up a date through text, you should never ASK a girl to go out on a date. Forget about "Being a gentleman." You must make it seem like a mutual decision.

You need to be the dominant male and ask a girl to JOIN you or make the assumption that she wants to see you. When you ASK the girl out, it subconsciously sounds like the date is going to be boring or awkward.

For example, don't say, "Hey, you want to go out on a date with me Saturday night?" or "Can I take you out Saturday night?". Instead, say, "Hey, you're pretty cool; we should hang out. I'm free Saturday night, you down?".

This shows dominance and the fact that it subconsciously sounds like you are going to have a good time.

Chapter 9:
Using Social Media

D ating is hard. Aside from getting her to go on a date with you, the other way to get a girl interested in you is by initiating conversations and using your social media skills to build rapport.

Here, we'll talk about different ways of building rapport that doesn't suck and possibly even develops an attraction. This also includes what social media platforms are the best for connection building, as well as how you can use them most efficiently.

What is Social Media?

Let's talk about what social media is. Basically, it's a platform that connects individuals through technology. For example, Facebook connects people through a network where users can share content, communicate with others and get updates on their friends' lives and activities. Twitter has a similar system, but it uses hashtags and short messages (140 characters or less).

On Instagram, there are no words or actual conversations. It's a way to present yourself visually to the world and share your day-to-day experiences by taking photos that are aesthetically pleasing in both form and content.

Nowadays, there are numerous social media platforms such as Pinterest, Tumblr, Snapchat, etc. But the four we've mentioned are the most popular and widely used, along with dating apps like Tinder.

But why spend time on social media at all? After all, if you're trying to get a girl's number so that you can further things in the real world, why not just meet her in person? Is there any reason to invest time on social media?

The truth is: Social media is an excellent way to get a girl's attention for online dating or even to initiate contact with her if she's already your friend. Social media allows you to meet women without having to leave the house. All you need is a strong profile, a good-looking photo, and well-written posts.

Benefits of Social Media

The benefits of having a social media presence are vast, to say the least:

- It allows you to connect with girls you like directly without having to go through intermediaries (like mutual friends).
- It provides you the opportunity to display your personality to the world and show off your identity – both of which are excellent for attracting girls.
- It can help build rapport with girls that may not have been possible under normal circumstances. After all, it is a way to connect with them virtually. Even if you didn't know each other previously, social media could allow you to become friends or even start dating.
- It can give you an extra edge should you be communicating with a girl whom you want to meet in real life. It might even serve as proof that you actually like her. For example, if you're trying to convince her that she's wrong about something and she sees how assertive/friendly you are on social media

through photos, this could win her over and make her more amenable to meeting up in the real world for a date.

Get Started Today

I know it's hard, but it will pay off in the long run.

The idea is simple: You start your profile and post some photos of yourself so that girls will know who they're talking to when they see your profile name or name tag.

You also create a strong and attractive profile picture, preferably one that is as visually appealing as possible. Take your profile as a business card. You want her to see that you're handsome, confident, smart, interesting, and confident. You must really believe in yourself so that she will too.

When you post your first update/photo, be sure to make yourself sound interesting enough so that she'll want to know more about you. This means talking about something or sharing something interesting with her that applies to either you or the group she's in (community) so that it's not just random chat talk. For example, if your friend is in the army, a photo of military vehicles or soldiers could work.

You can also talk about experiences in your life or things that you did recently. You don't have to be boring or over-talkative though. Just make sure your updates are relevant to what you're writing and what she's about so that she feels like she really knows you.

You should also link her profile with yours so that she can follow/find you and vice versa. This will ensure that when they see each other in person, they know where each other are coming from and what "type of people" they'll be dealing with.

Finally, make sure your updates are unique and interesting without being over-the-top or too provocative.

Once you get the hang of things, you can start making connections with girls, building rapport, and possibly deepening it into a relationship. Also, remember that these methods are great for developing attraction in women, so you're on the right track if they seem to be liking what they see.

You won't know when you've succeeded until they send you a message, tell you something about themselves, or even ask you out on a date.

Hows

<u>How to know if she's using this too and how to make your social media presence interesting to women</u>

At first, some people just want to see what's the big deal about social media. They don't have any interest in meeting up in real life or convincing anyone that they're interested in them; they just want to see what all the hype is about and how it can help them meet guys.

The problem with this is that there really isn't much of a secret social media "goldmine" for guys at the moment.

The only real way you can tell if a girl uses social media to find guys is to look at their profile. If you notice that she's too much of a premium user (e.g., has a lot of likes, follows, or fans), then it's very likely that she's using this method to try and "game" guys for dates, relationships, or even sex – which is something that needs to be avoided.

On the other hand, if you see that she has too little of these kinds of things going on, then it's not much of an indicator either way (because this could just mean the above point).

The only way you can really tell is to find out more about her and see if she seems open to the idea of meeting up in the real world or expressing interest in you. If not, then just move on.

If you're interested in making your social media presence interesting to women, then make sure that your updates reflect your personality and that they are funny while still being intriguing (not too provocative or sexual) so that they're worth checking out when the girls see them. The same goes for photos. If you're using photos of other people (like friends),m then make sure that they'll attract a girl's attention enough for them to want to check you out for themselves.

How to know if she wants to meet up in real life (make a date)

If you follow the above advice and make yourself interesting on social media, then you'll have the opportunity to ask a girl out on a date. Whether or not she accepts is another thing, but at least you've tried. It's also likely that if she's interested in meeting up with guys, then she will be open to talking about it with you.

Some of these indicators can be obvious – i.e., her commenting on your picture or video, liking it, and then sending you a message. If she does this, then it lends itself to an easy transition into an actual conversation about meeting up in person (via text message or social media).

Similarly, if she's commenting on your posts on her wall, her friends' walls, and making comments that are similar to the way she would comment on your photo/video if she wanted to meet up – then this is also a good sign.

Then there are the not-so-obvious signs like her inviting you to events that she's going to or ones that you can both go to. If she's really into meeting up with other guys, then she'll make it as much about you finding someone as it is about her finding someone. She'll be more than happy to set you up with another female friend of hers and so on and so forth.

Yes, this might, on some occasions, feel like she's just being nice, but even if that's the case – it still means that there's a decent chance that you'll be able to meet up with her in person at some point in the future.

It might also mean that you're being set up in a platonic way for someone else who would like to meet you too. After all, most people don't want to be set up with their friends' ex-girlfriends, and so it's a very nice way for someone else to let you know about them. It's just polite, really.

What Social Media Platforms to Use

1. Facebook

Facebook is one of the social media platforms famous for attracting women and initiating conversation with them. It has a very user-friendly interface, which makes it ideal for anyone interested in using its features.

You can use Facebook to meet new people or reconnect with old friends as well (and this last point is something that you should keep in mind). If you're already using Facebook to connect with your female friends, then great. If not, then you better start now!

All you need is a profile picture (preferably showing only your face) and a strong title (that's also eye-catching). These are the two things that people tend to look at first when they see your profile name or name tag, and so it's important that they work for you.

You can also post updates that will attract attention from other users based on the posts you make. Be sure to do this in a fun way as well so that she thinks she's getting some good entertainment value out of your updates.

You'll be able to connect with other girls on Facebook easily – just like the rest of the world does – but try not to overdo it with people who don't really give a damn about you. This is just common courtesy and shows that you're not materialistic.

If you want to make things easier, you can also create an entirely unconnected profile on Facebook and then start using it for updates, photos and posts only once you get more comfortable with the platform.

Another thing you can do is add her to your existing company's Facebook account. This will help you to connect with her seamlessly and will allow her to see all your updates when she goes online through that account.

You can also use Facebook as a platform for teasing girls that you're interested in because there are many memes, jokes, and articles about how good it is to keep a girl waiting (for example, have them wait for your approval before they talk with them). If a girl likes the fact that other girls are on there waiting for you to come online and approve them, then she'll be more likely to talk with you.

2. Twitter

Twitter is another platform that will help you connect with plenty of people from all over the world. It's also extremely visual, so you can actually show off photos and videos that you post. It is likewise a great platform you can use to impress people because it has very little text, and much emphasis is put on images.

It can be a very fun way of communicating with girls too, especially if they're interested in meeting up in real life with some guys (although this doesn't work for everyone). If you're using it to connect with girls, then you'll be able to follow them without them knowing, and they'll see that you're following them (as long as your account isn't private).

Just like on Facebook, you can also use Twitter as a platform for teasing girls too – if they're into it of course! For example, send out tweets that will cause them to react:

I love your shirt. 3 day notice? #tuesday

I just got back to work from vacation wearing the same underwear I packed 3 years ago. #tuesday

I'm having a sleepover with the weatherman. Wish me luck. #tuesday

3. Instagram

Instagram is another visual platform that has a lot of users around the world. It's also very flexible too because it allows you to post all kinds of photos, and not just pictures: video, short clips, memes, quotes, and anything else you can think of. It's also easy to share photos and videos from other social media sites like Facebook so that you don't have to take them from your phone.

Instagram is probably the most popular social media site for guys to use when it comes to attracting women because of how beautiful and appealing it can be when used correctly. It's a great way of showing girls that you're stylish, like fashion, and also have good taste when it comes to girls (as well as yourself).

If you're using Instagram to connect with other girls, then you'll be able to follow them without having to tweet them first or even see their profile photos. You can also comment on all their photos, essentially commenting on them in a Facebook-like manner: by liking, commenting, or sharing one photo.

You can also choose a female profile to follow so that you get updates from her without having to search for them. If you're interested in making your Instagram account interesting for girls, then be sure to use it in a way as this above piece of advice suggests:

Like and comment on other girls' photos on Instagram. The more likes and comments, the more she'll want to check you out

4. Pinterest and Tumblr

When used correctly, these two social media sites can be very interesting platforms for attracting girls (provided that you're not being creepy or sexual). They're also visually engaging because they allow you to pin images that will draw her attention.

You can pin images of whatever you want to. You can make your Pinterest account interesting for girls by doing the following:

- Post inspirational quotes

- Post funny memes (there are a lot of these on the internet)
- Make collages of photos and pin them (you can even ask her if she likes specific pictures to put in) or put together an album with your favorite pictures of her and screenshots of conversation you've had with her. Don't forget to start a Pinterest board just for this! This is one helluva way to keep that connection going and make her want to see more.
- Pin cute animal pictures too – it doesn't matter whether they're kittens or dogs, etc. Be as creative as you want!

5. Snapchat

Snapchat is a social media platform for sending messages and photos to other people with the press of a button. You send the photos and videos as they're being taken, which means that the girls won't even know when they've been sent. It's kind of like an INSTANT message that doesn't count for anything. This might not be the best social media platform to use if you want to be noticed by girls because it doesn't provide them with any feedback regarding what happened when the messages are being sent (as opposed to other platforms).

You can post photos and videos that will be available to her in real-time. This is a great way to tease girls because they'll think that you're updating them on something, but they won't know what.

You can also use Snapchat to send the girls links to articles or funny pages on the internet. In fact, it's probably easier to do this on Snapchat than anywhere else because you don't even need her number (although it's helpful if you already have it). You just send the Snap, and then she has 30 seconds to view it before it disappears from her screen. If this sounds interesting, then have some fun and get right into it!

Chapter 10:

Handling the First Call

Many guys who get a number from a girl will only spend their time talking with the girl using text. While this is a way to go, if you really want to stand out, you need to make a call to the girl as well. It is going to take some confidence in order to make this call rather than hiding behind some texts. It is also a big risk to giving instance responses rather than getting some time to think about what you would like to say. Most men are going to be worried about what they should say and how do they make the conversation last rather than let it go flat. Follow some of these tips for that first phone call so it can go off without a hitch, and you can get that date.

The Pre-Call:

Before you start calling the girl, you should make sure that your game is on. Sometimes practicing out the things that you want to say before you call the girl, or at least having some sort of list present, can help you get this done easier without as many worries. Write some of these things down, and then have a practice conversation a few times before you call. This can really help if you have the jitters about talking to her and can keep you from slipping up as much during the conversation. Of course the conversation is not going to go exactly the way that you practiced it, but at least you have a little practice and are able to feel a bit more confident before starting.

Work On Your Voicemail

In some cases, the girl may give you a call first. If this does happen, you want to make sure that she will be interested in leaving you a voicemail. Have the message on your voicemail be funny or cute or even leave a little brain teaser. This allows you to have something to talk about when you give her a callback, which will avoid some of the awkward pauses that often come with the phone conversation.

When You Should Call

It is a good idea to call her at some point, but you will also want to make sure that she is available and that you will not be bugging her, and you want to be able to ask her out on a date with plenty of time for preparations, so it does not sound like it was planned last minute. Some of the things that you can keep in mind when you are looking to call a girl include:

Right after getting the phone number—it is sometimes a good idea to call a girl right after you have gotten her number. This helps you to stay in her mind a bit longer, and you can just start it out with making sure that you got the right number. If possible, start the conversation where you left off when you last met to keep things interesting.

Sunday to Wednesday—the best time to call is in between these days. The rest of the days are the ones when people are the busiest, and she will probably be out doing something else. You are going to seem a little pathetic if you are calling and wanting to talk for a long time on a Saturday night. You should also call earlier in the week if you are planning on asking her out so that she has plenty of time to have a clear schedule and can come out with you.

Send a text ahead of time—text the girl before you decide to call her to see if she is busy or available to talk for a while. This allows you to know that she is free and that you will not be bothering her as much as you would just calling on the fly. Of course, another fun thing to do is wait for her to text you because you will then automatically know that she is free and you will not be bothering her. When you receive that text, reply back that you are going to call her in a few seconds. Wait a minute or two and then call. Then she is expecting you to call, and you can get right into the conversation.

Set up your time early—you can even set up the time that you would like to call her as you are getting her number. You can tell her that you would be free on Monday night at 7 pm and see if that time will work for her. This allows you to have free time to call and can get rid of the anxiousness you might be feeling about her not answering the phone at all.

Ready For The Call

It is fine to be a bit nervous during this part of the process, but do not let the rings on the other end scare you. Some men might pick up the phone, but they are so nervous that they hope it will go straight to voicemail so that they do not have to talk to the woman. Take a big breath while you are calling, and start thinking more positively.

When it is the first time that you are calling, it is not a good idea to hang up the phone until it is done. This means that you either need to have a conversation with the girl, or you need to leave a voicemail. Hopefully, you are able to get in touch with the girl so that you can have a conversation and get to know each other, but at least with a voicemail, you are providing an incentive for her to get back to you.

If you do end up leaving a voicemail, make sure that you are doing it in the right way in order to entice her to give you a callback. You can leave almost anything that you would like ranging from a question you would like her to answer, saying something that is kind of crazy, or just mention your last conversation to pique her interest. You can also make the conversation sweet and to the point. Just make sure that you are not just asking her to call you back when she has the time. This does not put a limit on when she can call you, and it could take a week or could be when you are at work, and the phone tag will begin. If you have a certain time that would work best for you, tell her to make things easier.

In some cases, the woman might not be able to call you back for a few days. She might have something going on or might not have realized that there was a message for her. If you do not get a callback, you should wait a few days before trying to call her again.

She Picks It Up

In some cases, the woman is going to actually pick up the phone when you call her. Do not take this as a bad sign. It was exactly what you wanted. But if she does pick up, make sure that you have something to say. You do not want to make the conversation awkward or end up hanging up the phone on her. This goes back to having a few ideas ready and written down, so even if you get stuck, you can help yourself out. You also need to make sure that you are able to keep the conversation going for a while; no one wants to just have a conversation that is a question and then a few word answer. Try to talk about something that interests you as well as her or imagine that you are talking to one of your good friends. The woman will respond in kind, and then the conversation will keep going for a long period of time. Of course, you also need to make a good way to end the conversation since it is not going to go on forever. You could say that you have something going on that you need to go do or even set up the date to end out the call.

As you can see, the phone call with the girl does not have to be as scary as you think. She is as worried about how this will go as you are, so just take a deep breath and have some fun. It does not have to be tedious and can even be an extension of the foundation you have worked on with the texting. Plus, it is going to put you in a much better light with this woman, which can make the whole date go so much better.

Conclusion

H aving good phone skills is important because it will facilitate and increase the chances of her meeting you for a date after the initial interaction. Your phone skills are important, but they pale in significance compared with the most important thing, and that is to become a more attractive guy in general.

When you are that guy, your phone game won't even matter that much because the girl will want to see you again. Having said that, here are some important things to remember about phone skills.

Girls give out their numbers all the time. Don't take the act of her giving you her number as any guarantee. It doesn't mean much and is only just a potential at this stage.

Just like girls give out their number a lot, they also flake a lot. Her flaking can be because she was not attracted to you enough or for a multitude of other reasons that are beyond your control. Don't over-analyze the scenario as to why it happened.

The only thing you should be focused on is whether you yourself were attractive enough when you met her and how you will be with the next girl.

When you get her number, text her your name right away or shortly after. She'll know who you are when you text her next. Then over the next few days, send her ping texts that show a playful side to you and keep you on her radar. Avoid texts that convey desperation and that you really want to meet her.

Show her that you're not rushing for the date. Demonstrate abundance and non-neediness. Find the balance between showing enough interest but not making her the most important thing that has happened to you recently.

After a few days of texting here and there, suggest a meet-up. Also, stick to texts instead of calling. Calling runs more risk that you will mess up and turn her off.

When you set up the date, suggest a good date idea and give her 2 options for days. If she agrees to one, set it for that day and lead by telling her when and where to meet. If she is vague and doesn't seem too interested, leave it for now. Act unaffected and like it's no big deal to you. Ping her 2-3 days after and try again. If she's still not showing interest, let her go.

When you do set up a date, text her a couple of hours before to remind her, and tell her that you'll be 15 minutes late. This will give her an opportunity to tell you that she can't make it. She'll only do it if she was already thinking about it; you're just bringing it up to the surface. You're saving yourself from wasting time and showing up to nothing.

If she does flake on you and lets you know in advance that she won't show up, don't be reactive. Act as if it's nothing. Don't ask when she's available next. Let her chase you. If she doesn't, then you don't have much chance with her. Think abundance and let her go.

Your main focus should always be on becoming a more attractive guy, not on getting that one girl.

We hope that you found this eBook helpful on how to turn a number into a date. Remember that your mindset is more important than the specific wording of the text. There is no magic line if you're not an attractive guy, to begin with. Having said that, when you are an attractive guy, having good phone game will help you and increase the chances that she'll come on a date with you.

Thanks for reading this book. I really hope you enjoyed it, and if you haven't yet, could you kindly leave this book a review on Amazon?

I really appreciate your review. Thank you.

CPSIA information can be obtained
at www.ICGtesting.com
Printed in the USA
BVHW061245020621
608544BV00005B/1400

9 781914 527555